ART from the HEART

The Ricky Trione Story

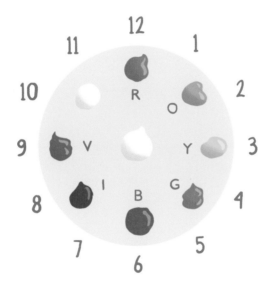

Written by
Karyn W. Tunks

Illustrated by
Nidhom

Featuring art by
Ricky Trione

ISBN 978-0-9711404-2-4

Printed in Korea
First Edition

SBA Books
P.O. Box 3019
Daphne, AL 36526

To God we give the Glory!

Ricky is different from most artists.

Other artists like to work alone,
with no one around to distract them.

They create art in secluded studios, out-of-the-way attics, or in secret rooms behind closed doors.

But not Ricky.

He learned when he was just a little boy that creating art was meant to be shared with others.

Ricky was part of a large family.
He grew up with:

1 brother
1 sister
2 parents
2 great-grandparents
4 grandparents
15 aunts
19 uncles AND
39 cousins **!**

It was exciting to have so many relatives living nearby!
There was always someplace to go and something to do.

Ricky liked to tag along behind the older boys. But when the fun and games turned to pulling pranks and double-dog-dares, Ricky quietly slipped away to spend time with his favorite uncle.

Uncle Ronald greeted all his visitors with a warm smile and cheerful hello. He was a talented artist and always happy to share with others his unique method of painting.

Ricky loved to watch as his uncle held a paintbrush tightly between his teeth. Unable to move his arms or hands, Uncle Ronald painted by moving only his head and neck. It took skill and effort. Ricky admired his uncle's talent and wanted to be an artist, too.

Soon Ricky had his own pad of paper, ink pens, and drawing pencils. He learned to sketch objects and scenes, always in shades of black and gray. And though Ricky was just a beginner, Uncle Ronald never corrected him. Instead, he encouraged his nephew to create art in his own way and to never give up.

Ricky practiced every day and took art classes in school. He sketched detailed images that showed his love of living near the bay.

Sand Island Light

Rick Trione 88

Rick Trione

Rick Trione

Rick Trione

Ricky grew up and became an officer in the United States Army. He married Bonnie, his childhood sweetheart. They had two sons and one daughter.

All three children watched their father sketch, and
one-by-one they began to draw in their own sketchbooks.
Ricky was proud to pass along the tradition of creating art
with people he loved. He felt like the luckiest person in the
whole world.

Then, in a flash, everything changed. There was a terrible accident and Ricky lost his sight.

His world turned dark and gray.

When the doctor said he would never see again, Ricky was mad, scared, and sad. He felt sorry for himself that something so unfair had happened. But Ricky had no other choice. He had to adjust to living as a blind person.

He practiced using a white cane until he could safely walk without bumping into objects.

He taught himself to read by touching raised dots on a page, a reading code known as Braille.

"It is eight thirty a.m."

He learned to use talking devices to make it easier to do everyday tasks.

Gradually, with hard work and prayer Ricky learned how to live without his eyesight. He swallowed his pride and accepted help from family and friends. He stopped focusing on what was lost and made a choice to live with gratitude.

With his new, can-do attitude, Ricky's life began to change for the better and unexpected opportunities came his way.

One day, a friend offered to help Ricky get back to work as an artist. But how could he create art without his sight? Ricky thought it was a crazy idea but was ready to give it a try. They began experimenting with new techniques and materials.

Ricky realized that drawing with crayons left a wax film on the paper, which he could feel with his fingers.

Lines squeezed from bottles of glue and special paints dried with a raised texture.

His pointer finger could be used as a paintbrush, filling in lines with bright paints arranged on a round palette.

After a lot of practice and determination, Ricky was creating art, again!

Go Against the Flow

Jacy's Sunflower

Choose Your Battles

"Choose Your Battles" Ricky Trione

What happened next was something Ricky never expected. A teacher invited him to show her students how he created art. He was excited but very nervous. What would the children think about an artist who was blind? What if he made a mistake? Ricky decided to be brave and agreed to go.

There was no reason for Ricky to worry. The children were kind, encouraging and very excited about creating their own art. From that day on, he became "Mr. Ricky."

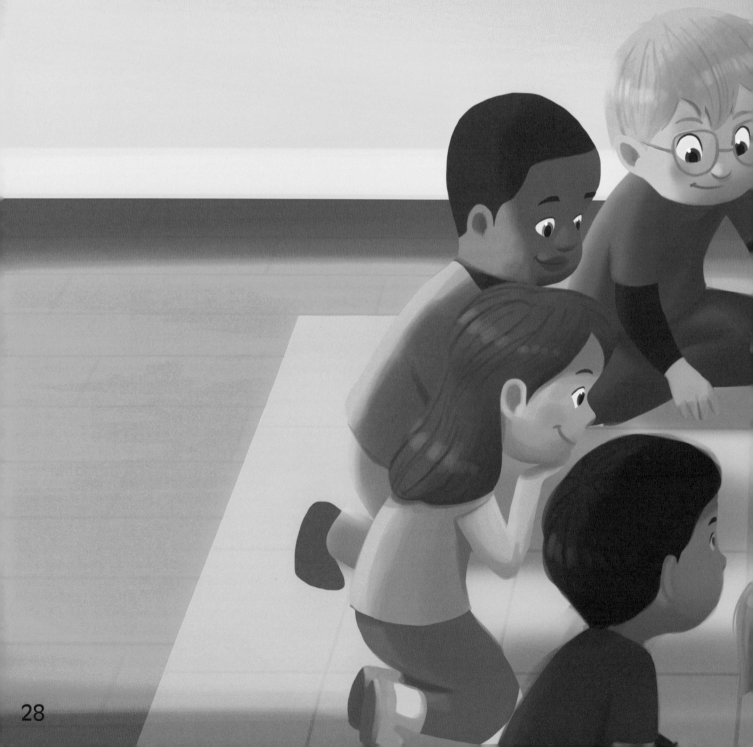

Since that first school visit, Mr. Ricky has shared his method of creating art with hundreds of people of all ages. He feels blessed to be an artist who can pass on the lessons he learned as a young boy…

creating art is meant to be shared with others and no matter what, never, ever give up!

The End

Ask Mr. Ricky: In-depth Answers to Commonly Asked Questions

Why was your Uncle Ronald in a wheelchair?
The summer before Ronald Trione's senior year in high school, he went swimming with friends. He dove off the pier into shallow waters of Mobile Bay and struck his head on the bottom, breaking his neck. Ronald became a quadriplegic, and he was unable to move his arms and legs from then until his death at 30 years old. Ronald was only able to turn his head from side-to-side and up and down. My grandmother taped objects to a stick-like tool that Ronald held with a mouthpiece. He could turn a book's pages by using an eraser, and play Checkers by touching this tool to the piece he wanted moved. My grandmother enrolled him in a correspondence art course where he learned how to paint. This gave his life greater purpose. Ronald never dwelled on his limitations but remained cheerful and positive his entire life.

How did you lose your sight?
I had two accidents over seven years that took my vision away, one eye at a time. My left eye was permanently damaged when I was a Captain in the Army in 1993. While driving during maneuvers, a rock was slung through an open window and hit me in the eye. Then, seven years later, I had car trouble and pulled over on the side of the road; a big semi-truck passing by had a blowout and a large strip of belted tire tread hit me in the other eye, making me blind.

How did you come up with the idea for arranging paint colors on the round palette?
At first, white paint and the primary colors—red, yellow and blue—were put anywhere on my round palette. Someone always had to be with me to tell me what paint color I was using from my palette. During one school visit, we were doing rainbow art. I admitted I did not know the order of the colors in the rainbow and asked if any of the students could tell me. A third-grade girl gave me a lesson I'll never forget! "Mr. Ricky!" she scolded, "you are too old not to know the order of the colors in the rainbow. All you have to do is remember the name, ROY G. BIV." She explained that ROY stands for red, orange, and yellow, G is for green and BIV means blue, indigo, and violet. It was like a light bulb turned on in my brain: I had one of those wonderful "WOW" moments! I now use the name ROY G. BIV to set up the colors of paints on my palette like a clock and now can paint all by myself: I put red paint at 12 o'clock, yellow at 3 o'clock, blue at 6 o'clock and white in the very middle. From there, I can mix other colors. I've taught this method to many others, including children and adults who are sight impaired. I am so grateful for that third-grader and her lesson on ROY G. BIV!

How did your artistic style change after losing your sight?
I grew up loving to draw with pencil and eventually pen and ink. All my work was in black and white! I took colors for granted and did not appreciate them as much as I do today. People think I live in darkness, but when I started learning how to express myself through art as a blind person my world became very colorful with many vibrant and happy hues. It was my childhood friend, Vicky Nix Cook, who persuaded me to begin creating art again and she was also the person responsible for my first school visits. I use different materials and tools now, such as school glue, when I want lines to appear as if they are off in the distance or to fill in an area to make it more raised. Puff paint is my favorite paint to draw with because it makes thick raised lines when it dries and it's available in many colors. My wife, Bonnie, helps me experiment with other materials, such as tubes of caulking and drywall compound, which creates textured images in a style called "relief."

How do you visualize what you are drawing and painting?
Since I am no longer able to look at a scene or photograph to create a composition, I have to recall the shapes and colors of familiar objects. This has become an inspiration for me; my creations became alive in my mind and on the canvas with beautiful, vibrant colors. Blue crabs are embellished in vibrant turquoise, seafoam green, and splashes of bright red in the background, with many shades of greens and blues. Sometimes I create colorful blue crabs with bright orange backgrounds and others with violet purple. I call this creating art from the heart!

What message do you want to share with others who have to overcome obstacles and barriers?
My message is: When facing difficult obstacles in life, be humble enough to allow others to help and teach you rather than relying on just your own strength. When I became blind, I was too proud to ask for, or accept, any help. After I humbled myself and let people into my life who offered their help, many blessings started coming my way through friendships with caring and loving people. Through my difficult circumstances, I realized that God had been sending His loving people to help me each step of the way. The greatest life lesson for me is learning to "walk by faith not by sight."(2 Corinthians 5:7) And this is what I practice each moment of each day.